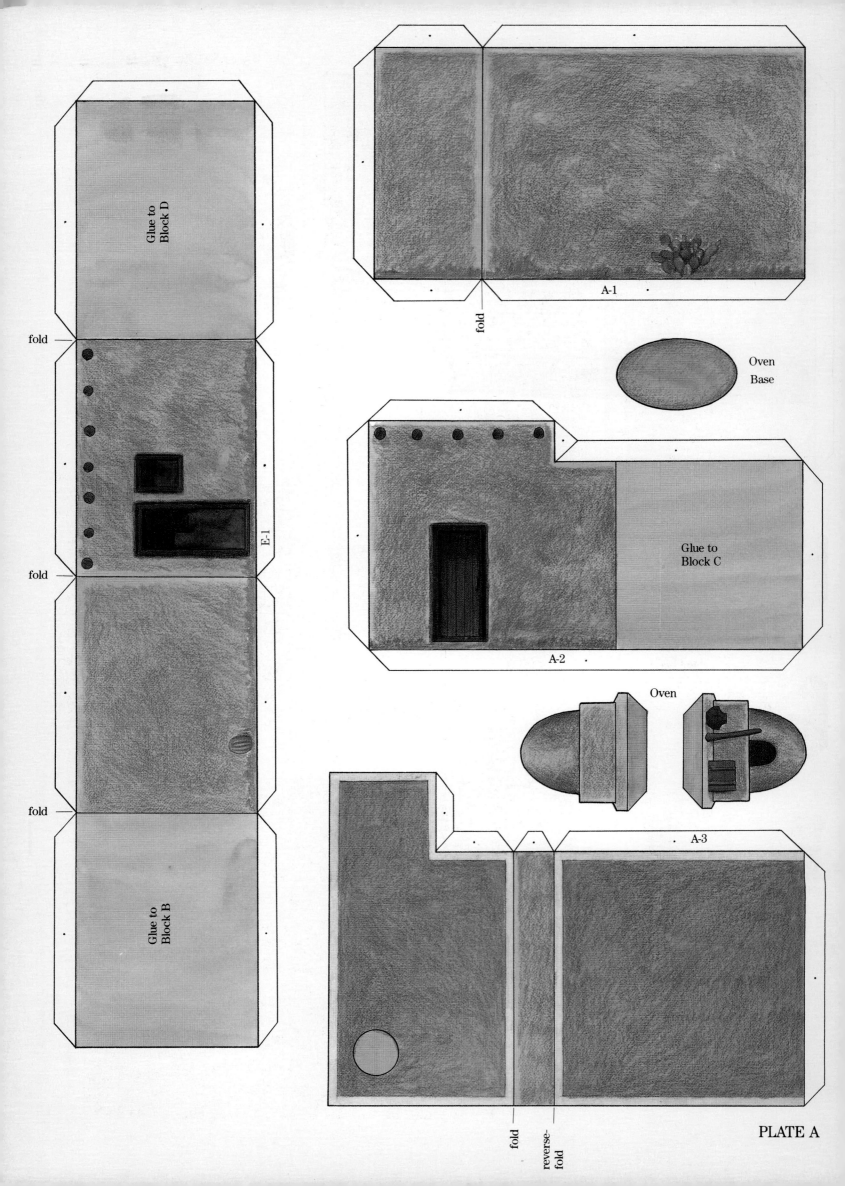

Glue to
Block D

fold

E-1

fold

fold

Glue to
Block B

A-1

fold

Oven
Base

Glue to
Block C

A-2

Oven

A-3

fold

reverse-
fold

PLATE A

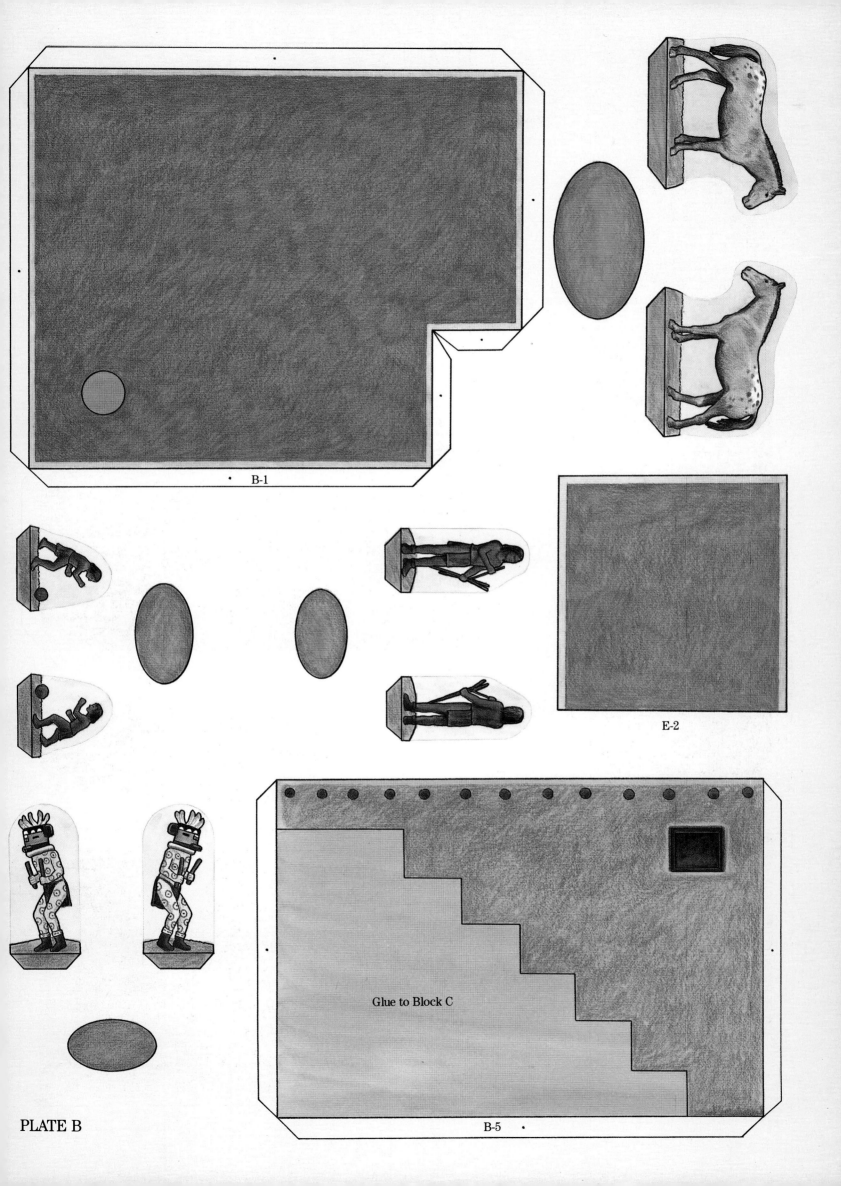

B-1

E-2

Glue to Block C

PLATE B

B-5

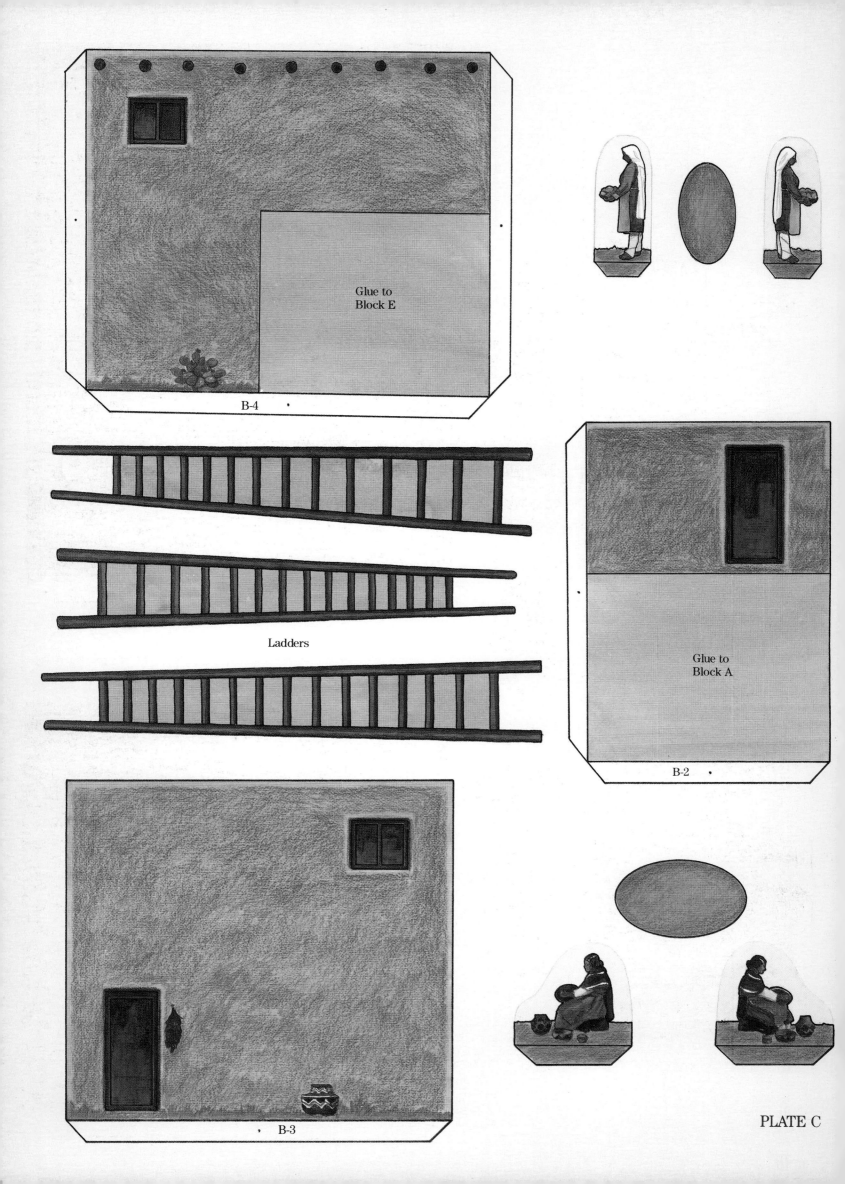

Glue to
Block E

B-4

Ladders

Glue to
Block A

B-2

Glue to
Block A

B-3

PLATE C

C-1

fold
fold
fold
fold
fold
fold
fold
fold
fold
fold

PLATE D

D-5

Glue to Block B

Glue to Block A

D-4

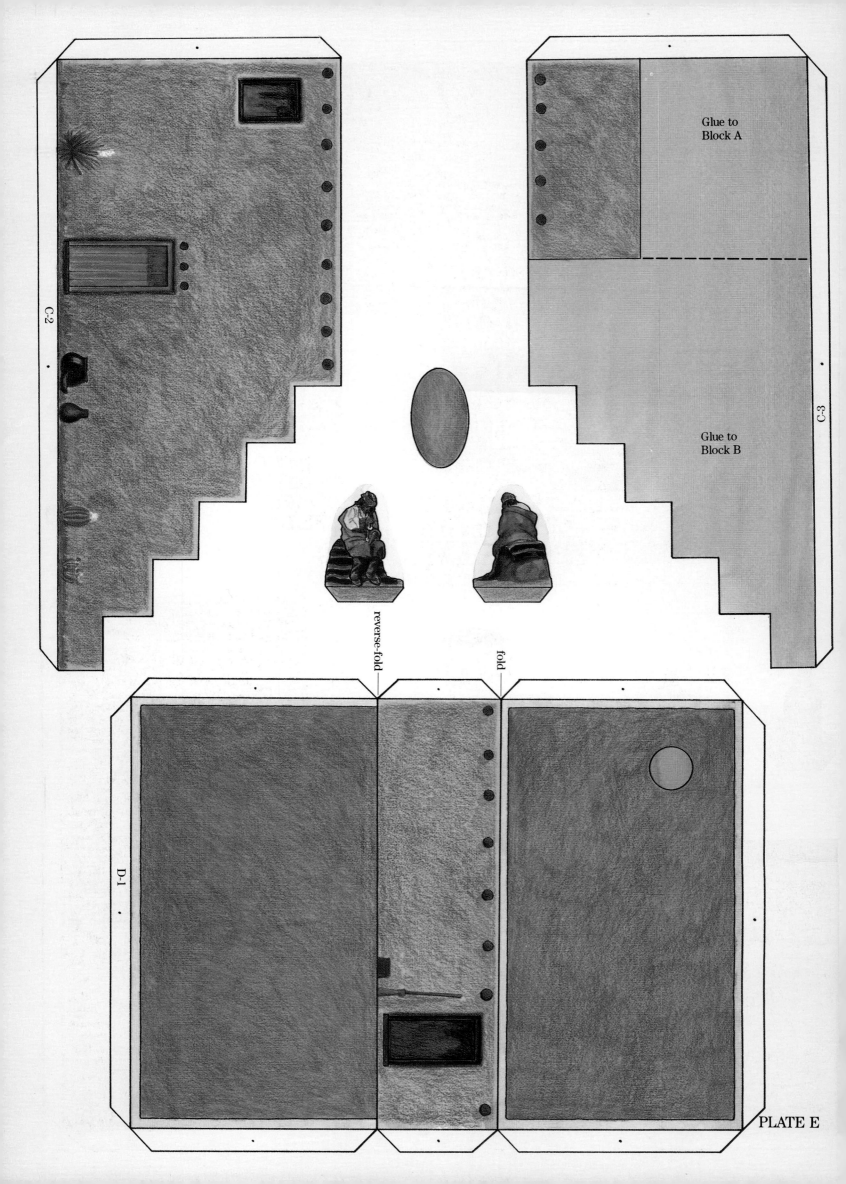

C-2

C-3

Glue to
Block A

Glue to
Block B

reverse-fold

fold

D-1

PLATE E

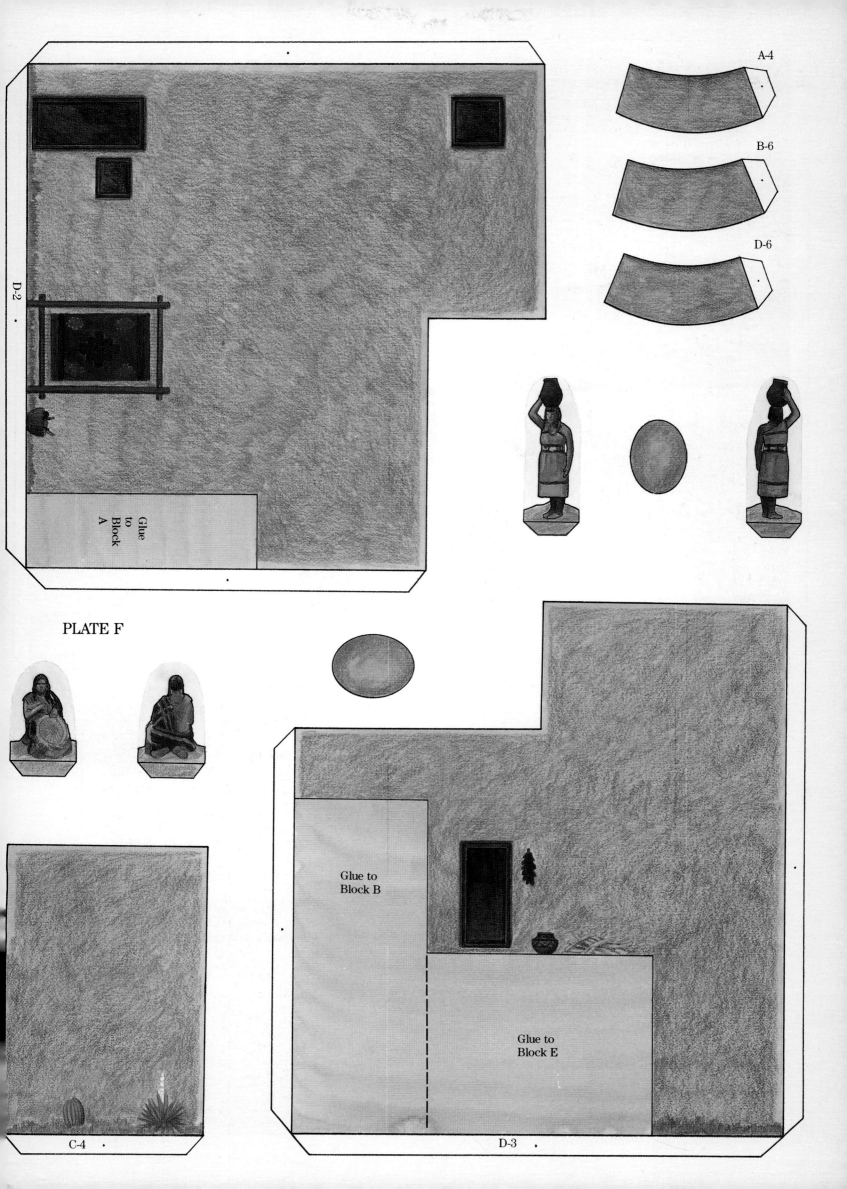

A-4

B-6

D-6

D-2

Glue
to
Block
A

PLATE F

Glue to
Block B

Glue to
Block E

C-4

D-3

(continued from inside front cover)

a slight groove in the paper, but not so hard that you cut through it. The reverse-folded lines should be reverse-scored, that is, scored on the *underside* of the paper.

Now carefully cut out the pieces for Block A. Try them carefully for fit before applying any glue. When you are sure that the pieces are in their proper places, carefully glue them together. When applying glue to a tab, apply it *only* to the tab, not the receiving surface. Do not use too much glue or it will seep out and cause a mess. Keep a damp tissue or sponge handy for wiping away any excess glue. Use a spoon or similar tool to press down the parts that have been glued together. Pause between steps to allow the glue to dry.

After the five blocks have been assembled and the glue has dried, fit them together as shown in the diagrams and on the cover. When you are sure that you know how they are supposed to go, glue them together as marked. Allow all the pieces to dry.

Meanwhile, you can assemble the stand-up figures. Each is made of two parts that are glued back-to-back. Before you glue these parts together, reverse-score the lines along the tabs at the bottom. These tabs are glued to the base, the oval-shaped piece near each figure in the book. Finally, cut out the ladders. A suggestion for placing these is given in the second diagram. Notice the various activities in which the figures are engaged. The figures may be arranged around the pueblo and on its roofs to create a realistic setting (a suggested arrangement is shown in the photo on the front cover). Have fun!

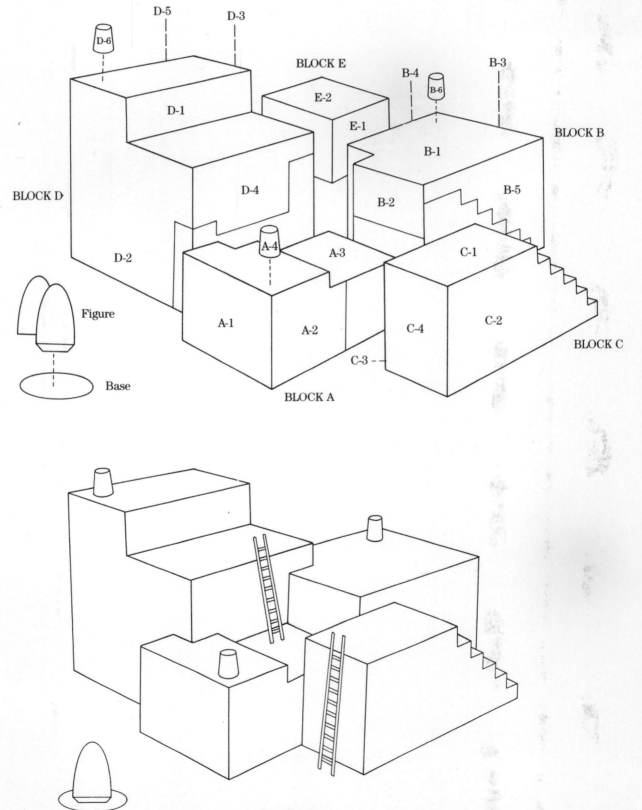

Completed